The Essential SIMON & GARFUNKEL

D0863046

Amsco Publications
New York/London/Paris/Sydney/Tokyo/Berlin/Copenhagen/Madrid

Photography
front cover: Don Hunstein/Sony Music Archives
back cover: © Bettmann/CORBIS
page 2: Guy Webster

Order No. PS 11583
US International Standard Book Number: 0.8256.3322.2
UK International Standard Book Number: 1.84449.338.5

Exclusive Distributors:
Music Sales Corporation
257 Park Avenue South, New York, NY 10010 USA
Music Sales Limited
8/9 Frith Street, London W1D 3JB England
Music Sales Pty. Limited
120 Rothschild Street, Rosebery, Sydney, NSW 2018, Australia

Printed in the United States of America by
Vicks Lithograph and Printing Corporation

Wednesday Morning, 3 A.M.

Words and Music by PAUL SIMON

Moderately bright

1. I can hear the soft breath-ing of the girl that I
2. (She is) soft, she is warm,___ but my heart re-mains

love,___ As she lies here be-side me a-
heav-y,___ And I watch as her breasts gent-ly

6

I held up and robbed __ a hard __ liq - uor

The morn - ing is

store. _____ 4. My

just a few hou - - rs _____ a -

way. _____

Bleecker Street

Words and Music by PAUL SIMON

shad - ow's hand,
pays   your   rent,   } On Bleeck   er___
Ca -   naan,

Street.

play three times

Mm,_____   Ooh,

The Sound Of Silence

Words and Music by PAUL SIMON

Leaves That Are Green

Words and Music by PAUL SIMON

Moderately

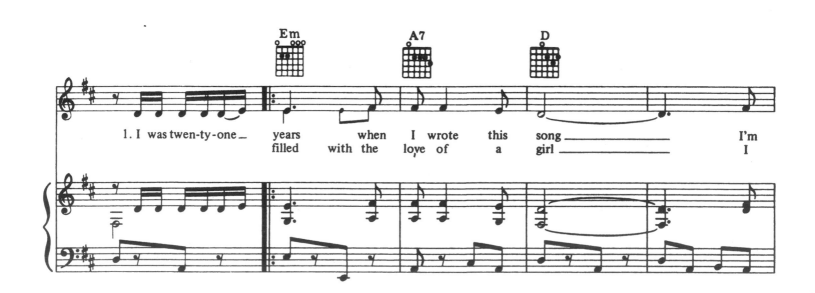

1. I was twen-ty-one __ years when I wrote this song _____ I'm
filled with the love of a girl _____ I

A Most Peculiar Man

Words and Music by PAUL SIMON

never wake up To his si - lent world ___ and his tin - y room; ___ And

Mis - sus Rior - don says he has a broth - er some- where ___ Who should be

no - ti - fied ___ soon. ___ And all the peo-ple said, "What a

shame that he's dead, But was - n't he A Most Pe - cul - iar Man?" ___

Richard Cory
Words and Music by PAUL SIMON

I Am A Rock

Words and Music by PAUL SIMON

Kathy's Song
Words and Music by PAUL SIMON

Homeward Bound
Words and Music by PAUL SIMON

Scarborough Fair/Canticle

Arrangement and original counter melody by PAUL SIMON and ARTHUR GARFUNKEL

40

Sparrow

Words and Music by PAUL SIMON

far _____ and cries for rest? _____
speak _____ a kind - ly word? _____
feed _____ a starv - ing spar - row? _____
write _____ her eu - lo - gy? _____

"Not I," said the oak tree, _____
"Not I," said the swan, _____
"Not I," said the gold - en wheat, _____
"I will," said the earth, _____

"I won't share my branch - es with
"The en - tire _____ i - dea _____ is
"I would if I could but I
"For all I've cre - a - ted re -

44

The 59th Street Bridge Song
(Feelin' Groovy)

Words and Music by PAUL SIMON

The Dangling Conversation

Words and Music by PAUL SIMON

still life wa-ter col-or, _____ of a now late af-ter-
read your Em-'ly Dick-in-son, _____ and I my Rob-ert
speak of things that mat-ter, _____ with words that must be

A Hazy Shade Of Winter
Words and Music by PAUL SIMON

A Poem On The Underground Wall

Words and Music by PAUL SIMON

At The Zoo
Words and Music by PAUL SIMON

64

Old Friends

Words and Music by PAUL SIMON

Mrs. Robinson
Words and Music by PAUL SIMON

D.S. al Coda

Coda

Verse:

G   G7

2. Hide it in a hid - ing place where
3. Sit - ting on a so - fa on a

no one ev - er goes,
Sun - day af - ter - noon,

C 7

Put it in your pan - try with your cup - cakes,
Go - ing to the can - di - dates' de - bate,

F 7   Bb

It's a lit - tle se - cret, just the Rob -
Laugh a - bout it, shout a - bout it,

God bless you, please, Mrs. ___ Rob - in - son, ___
What's that you say, Mrs. ___ Rob - in - son, ___

Heav - en holds ___ a place ___ for those ___ who pray. ___
"Jolt - in' Joe" ___ has left and gone ___ a - way. ___

(Hey, hey, hey, _____ hey, hey, hey. ___
(Hey, hey, hey, _____ hey, hey, hey. ___

Fakin' It

Words and Music by PAUL SIMON

Take the time to treat your friend-ly neigh-bors hon-est-ly,___

I've just been Fak-in' it, Fak-in' it, Not real-ly

mak-in' it; This feel-in' of Fak-in' it,

I still have-n't shak-en it.___

Bookends

Words and Music by PAUL SIMON

America
Words and Music by PAUL SIMON

board - ed a Grey - hound in Pitts - burgh, _____

_____ "Mich - i - gan seems like a dream to me now. _____

_____ It took me four days To hitch - hike from

Sag - i - naw. I've come _____ to look for A - mer -

Overs

Words and Music by PAUL SIMON

El Condor Pasa
(If I Could)

English Lyric by PAUL SIMON
Musical arrangement by JORGE MILCHBERG and DANIEL ROBLES

Bridge Over Troubled Water

Words and Music by PAUL SIMON

Cecilia
Words and Music by PAUL SIMON

Moderate, not too fast, rhythmically

Keep The Customer Satisfied
Words and Music by PAUL SIMON

So Long, Frank Lloyd Wright

Words and Music by PAUL SIMON

Baby Driver

Words and Music by PAUL SIMON

Moderate bright tempo

1. My dad-dy was a fam-i-ly bass - man, My ma-
2. (My) dad-dy was a prom-i-nent frog - man, My ma-
3. (My) dad-dy got a big pro-mo - tion, My ma-

ma was an en-gi - neer, ___ And I ___ was born ___ one dark
ma's in the Na-val re - serve, ___ When I ___ was young ___ I car-
ma got a raise in pay, ___ There's no ___ one home, ___ we're all

The Boxer

Words and Music by PAUL SIMON

122

Song For The Asking

Words and Music by PAUL SIMON

For Emily, Whenever I May Find Her

Words and Music by PAUL SIMON

cheeks flushed with the night. We walked on

frost - ed fields _ of ju - ni - per and lamp - light,

I _ held your hand. _

And when I a - woke and felt you warm and near,

My Little Town

Words and Music by PAUL SIMON

In my lit-tle town ___ I grew up be-liev - ing

God keeps his eye ___ on us all.

And he used to lean ___ up-on ___ me as I pledged al - le - giance ___ to the

And af-ter it rains ____ there's a rain-

bow, and all of the col-ors are black. It's

not that the col-ors aren't there; it's just i-mag-i-na-

tion they ____ lack. Ev-'ry-thing's the same ____ back

The Only Living Boy In New York

Words and Music by PAUL SIMON